Dear Ann & Carl,

Thank you both for a wonderful trip — The New Mexico photo safari.

Best Wishes,
Charles
12/87

INDIANAPOLIS

Reflection of State Capitol Building in One North Capitol Building.

This book is dedicated to the memory of my father, Robert Shoffner, a gentleman from the Midwest.
Charles Shoffner

Fountain, University Park (*overleaf, pages 2-3*). Located in downtown Indianapolis, University Park is so named because it was originally intended to be the site for Indiana University-Purdue University at Indianapolis. Lockerbie Street (*overleaf, pages 4-5*). Shrine Room, Memorial Hall, World War Memorial Plaza (*overleaf, pages 6-7*). Memorial Hall is dedicated to Indiana citizens who gave their lives in the two World Wars, Korea, and Vietnam.

Designed by Josef Beery and Marilyn F. Appleby.
Edited by Kathleen D. Valenzi and Michael P. Spradlin.
Photographs copyright © 1987 by Charles Shoffner. All rights reserved.
Introduction copyright © 1987 by Tom Carnegie. All rights reserved.
This book, or any portions thereof, may not be reproduced or transmitted in any form or by any means, electronic or mechanical, including photocopying, recording, or by any information storage and retrieval system, without permission in writing from the publisher.
Photography may not be reproduced without permission of Charles Shoffner.
Introduction may not be reproduced without permission of Tom Carnegie.
Photograph pages 94-95 by Ron McQueeney. Printed courtesy of the Indianapolis Motor Speedway.
Library of Congress Catalog Card Number: 86-83146
ISBN 0-9616878-5-1
Printed and bound in Hong Kong by Everbest Printing Co., Ltd. for Four Colour Imports, Ltd., Louisville, Kentucky.
Published by Howell Press, Inc., 2000 Holiday Drive, Charlottesville, Virginia 22901.
Telephone (804) 977-4006.
First edition.
Spradlin-Patrick is an imprint of Howell Press, Inc.

SPRADLIN-PATRICK

INDIANAPOLIS

■

**Photography
Charles Shoffner**

**Introduction
Tom Carnegie**

INDIANAPOLIS

Suddenly, without trumpeting, Indianapolis has catapulted from a sleepy Indiana capital into a world-class city. Where progress was once glacially slow, more than $136 million has been invested in deluxe sports facilities. Another $1.5 billion has been spent on downtown construction projects, a huge sum for a city with a population of a little under 800,000. Indianapolis was host in 1984 to the world's largest indoor basketball crowd, when more than 67,000 fans cheered the men's and women's U.S. Olympic basketball teams—this in a city that once allowed its only major-league sports team, an N.B.A. basketball franchise, to go bankrupt.

Olympic-style is not the only basketball that generates excitement. Not to be overlooked is the frenzy caused by high-school basketball, an Indiana tradition since the early 1900s. The schoolboy game causes more excitement in Indiana than the annual *Sports Illustrated* swimsuit issue does nationally. The month-long, season-ending tournament draws nearly one and a half million spectators, and the state finals in Indianapolis have been a sellout for 57 consecutive years.

The key to the success of the high-school game in Indiana is that all teams go for a single state championship, despite wide disparity in enrollment. Hoosiers would have it no other way. Arsenal Technical of Indianapolis, once the state's largest school with over 5,000 pupils, has never won the crown. The most celebrated "small town" victory came in 1954 when the tiny school of Milan, boasting 150 in its student body, knocked off mighty Muncie Central to capture the title. The drama of that contest inspired the 1986 Hollywood movie *Hoosiers,* starring Gene Hackman, Barbara Hershey, and Dennis Hopper. Two Hoosier natives, Angelo Pizzo and David Anspaugh, wrote and directed the successful production.

Prep-school basketball is almost a religion in Indiana. "Hoosier Hysteria" is the one striking feature of the sports scene I most remember seeing when I first moved to Indianapolis from Missouri in the mid-1940s. Frankly, it was a shock. My first broadcasting challenge was to do radio play-by-play for eight games in a single day. Those eight games remain as my greatest broadcasting achievement, far

Indianapolis Motor Speedway and Hall of Fame Museum (*facing*). The Speedway Museum preserves the history of central Indiana's involvement in the nation's infant auto industry. From a small beginning in 1898, the industry grew rapidly. Within a few years, more than 256 makes of cars and trucks were being manufactured in Indiana—45 in Indianapolis alone.

more demanding than describing the three-and-a-half-hour, Indianapolis 500 race. With 17,000 screaming fans at Butler Fieldhouse (renamed in recent years for the legendary Paul D. "Tony" Hinkle), the experience left my nerves shattered and my confidence in my play-by-play abilities devastated. It was impossible to learn the players' names and numbers in advance, so I often resorted to vague expressions like "H-e-e-e-e made it!" to describe the spirited action.

The finest basketball player I've ever seen is Oscar Robertson, product of an all-black Indianapolis high school, Crispus Attucks. Robertson brought the Hoosier capital its first state high-school crown, added another, starred at the University of Cincinnati, won an Olympic Gold Medal, and then became a perennial N.B.A. All-Star.

Indianapolis has had the "Indy 500" since before World War I, but its fate hung in the balance in 1945 when WWI ace and former "500" driver Eddie Rickenbacker decided to sell the 570-acre racing complex. The decaying facility, neglected during World War II, was saved by Anton Hulman, Jr., a Terre Haute, Indiana, sportsman. Hulman pledged to reinvest any profits from the race in new grandstands and facilities. He also increased the prize money, which today totals more than $3 million.

It was the late Tony Hulman who started the city on its climb to world prominence, but his lead was not followed quickly. For a long time civic and government leaders seemed to prefer "Hoosier" Abe Martin's advice on investing: "The safest way to double your money is to fold it over once and put it in your pocket." Not until the early 1980s did Indianapolis discover its destiny, when civic leaders decided to make Indianapolis the "Amateur Sports Capital of the World."

Suddenly we had something to cheer, something to watch. In a few short years Indianapolis has become the only American city, other than Olympic host Los Angeles, that is fully equipped to handle a major international sports event. National television now makes frequent stops to cover our activities.

Revitalization of the city began in 1970 when a new state law brought Indianapolis and most of surrounding Marion County under a unified governing body. The plan quadrupled the city's land area to 378 square miles and boosted the tax base. It fostered a new "partnership" approach between government and the private sector in redeveloping the city.

That same year, the Amateur Athletic Union, which once controlled all amateur athletics in the United States, moved to Indianapolis from New York at the instigation of former Olympic swimmer, Frank McKinney, Jr. The Amateur Sports Act of 1978 later broke up the A.A.U., allowing individual sports to form independent national governing bodies in conformity with the rest of the world. Indianapolis saw a great opportunity and seized it. The

Indiana Sports Corporation was formed to attract the headquarters of the newly autonomous sports associations to the Hoosier capital.

Next, the Lilly Endowment stepped in. The Indianapolis-based foundation created by the Lilly family in 1937 identified five areas which needed funding in order for the city to become nationally competitive — culture, education, agriculture, health and medicine, and amateur athletics. Success was assured.

The love affair with amateur athletics began in 1983 when Indianapolis hosted the National Sports Festival, an event sponsored by the U.S. Olympic Committee. Crowds were tremendous. From the opening ceremony of the two-week competition — which featured more than 5,000 athletes in some two dozen sports — to the final event, the entire city was a frenzy of competitive activity.

Several sports facilities were already in place for use by the festival athletes. These included the Indianapolis Sports Center, a complex housing 24 tennis courts; the Indiana University Athletic Fields for softball, soccer, and volleyball; the Market Square Arena for sports, stage shows, ice skating, and gymnastics competitions; and the Major Taylor Velodrome for track bicycle racing.

The Indiana University Natatorium, undoubtedly the finest swimming complex in North America, was used during the festival, too. It boasts 4,700 spectator seats, two 50-meter pools, an 18-foot deep diving pool, and an auxiliary gymnasium. After the 1983 National Sports Festival, it was the site of the 1985 Synchronized Swimming World Cup Championships and of many of the U.S. Olympic trials, including swimming, diving, and synchronized swimming.

Another facility used for the festival was the Indiana University Track and Field Stadium, featuring a nine-lane, 400-meter rubber track. It was also the site of that year's National Track Championships. The festival made use of several other facilities, including Butler University's Hinkle Fieldhouse for basketball and the Convention Center for boxing, gymnastics, and other events.

The National Sports Festival firmly established Indianapolis as the "Amateur Sports Capital of the World." Several national sports association governing bodies moved their headquarters to the new amateur sports mecca. Among them were the Athletic Congress of the U.S.A. (track and field), the U.S. Diving Association, the U.S. Gymnastics Federation, the U.S. Rowing Association, the U.S. Synchronized Swimming Association, and the International Baseball Association.

Of these, the arrival of the U.S. Rowing Association caused the the greatest stir. Leaving Philadelphia's Boathouse Row and the shores of the Schuylkill River was heresy to some, but for the association, it was simply a good business decision. Indianapolis offered a Lilly Foundation grant for relocation expenses and new office facilities, as well as help with fund raising. The city also agreed to develop Eagle Creek Reservoir, located about 10 miles from town, into an internationally certified rowing course capable of accommodating a world championship.

Next came a new goal, a new dream. Civic leaders convinced Indianapolis taxpayers that a domed, 61,000-seat stadium built next to the Indiana Convention Center made economic sense, even though no sports tenant was lined up to occupy it. Soon after the Hoosier Dome was completed, however, the N.F.L. Colts signed a 20-year lease for use of the indoor facility. Indianapolis residents greeted the Colts' arrival with enthusiasm. In fact, response for season tickets was so great that fans had to enter a lottery to get them, leaving thousands of residents who did not make the draw on a waiting list.

Sports-inspired civic pride has had many positive side effects. In preparing for the arrival of national and international competitors, media, and guests, the city decided to brick in Monument Circle, an old landmark in the heart of downtown. Residents were given the opportunity to have their names inscribed on the bricks for $25 each. Trees, plants, lights, and park benches were then added to the area. The project marked the beginning of an expanding beautification process.

Indiana University-Purdue University at Indianapolis, with a student body of 23,000, is the state's third-largest university. Time and again, coaches of the university's natatorium would take me aside and preach the gospel of fitness through swimming. Finally, after ignoring their advice for many months, I began a regular swimming program. Dragging this 60-year-plus body, long ravaged by poor health habits, into a fitness class was a major hurdle. My progress was agonizingly slow, but persistence did pay off. Would you believe that two years after I started the program I won the 50-meter butterfly in the state's White River Park games? And I am only one of thousands of residents who have benefited from the natatorium's unique philosophy of making world-class swimming and exercise facilities open to the public.

Without question, athletics have sparked the development of Indianapolis' industry, housing, downtown, and future dreams. But athletics alone are not the sole attraction of this thriving, well-rounded community. The partnership philosophy has pumped an abundance of money and ideas into the city, resulting in more than two dozen major downtown renewal and construction projects for housing, office, convention, and cultural space. In the works is the $200-million White River State Park. When completed, the 250-acre park will feature a center for the performing arts, botanical gardens, restaurants, a 750-foot observation tower made of Indiana limestone, and the Indianapolis Zoo, home to 2,500 animals.

The cultural centerpiece of the city is the Indianapolis Museum of Art. Nestled amid 154 acres of beautiful grounds and botanical gardens, the museum's three art pavilions house treasures of yesteryear and today. Visitors enter a world of Old Master paintings and delicate orchids, of contemporary art and lush green pathways. The Krannert Pavilion contains many of the museum's major collections. It is home of the Eli Lilly Collection of Oriental Art, one of the most comprehensive collections of its kind in the United States — exhibiting five millenia of Chinese art in bronze, ceramics, jade, and paintings.

The Indianapolis Symphony Orchestra, founded in 1930, is one of the nation's major orchestras, with a budget of more than $6 million and a 50-week season. Built in 1916, the handsomely renovated Circle Theatre on Monument Circle became the home of the symphony in 1984. The old movie theater had previously lain idle after many residents moved out of the city and into the suburbs.

Another downtown movie and stage-show house from the past, the huge Indiana Theater, has been reclaimed as the home of the Indiana Repertory Theater. It houses three stages and a mammoth ballroom.

The Children's Museum in Indianapolis, started in 1925, is so unusual that it attracts 1.3 million visitors each year. The museum's exhibits cover five floors and display everything from dinosaur skeletons to the biggest toy train collection imaginable. With a staff of 180, aided by more than 500 volunteers, the museum averages 3,000 programs a year. Despite its growing sophistication, the museum remains a warm, accessible place that kids feel belongs to them.

Further north, through fine residential areas with beautiful trees, landscaped lawns, and an interesting variety of distinctive architecture, lies Butler University. With more than 4,000 students, the school has long enjoyed an international reputation in the performing arts. Clowes Hall, located on campus, is a major auditorium where distinguished concert artists and traveling stage shows appear each season. The delightful Starlight Theatre with its outdoor stage is a major summertime attraction.

The Hudson Institute, a world-famous "think tank," moved to Indianapolis from the suburbs of New York in 1984. When asked why they chose to move, Institute President Thomas D. Bell explained, "Indianapolis offers talent, leadership, cultural resources, a government structure willing to work to make things happen, and many fine universities offering faculty and facilities that broaden our research base." Their new home is a 32-room mansion isolated among acres of lawn and trees in the northeastern section of town.

Perhaps the most startling and daring venture of all is the $55-million restoration of century-old Union Station. The pride of the city before it was allowed to fall into disrepair, Union Station today retains its former grandeur. The giant complex—two city blocks long—was unveiled in 1986. One renovated section houses a collection of shops, restaurants, and nightclubs; the other contains a new 275-room hotel.

The dreams of the dreamers seem endless. New hotels are under construction. Old downtown factories and warehouses are being made into apartments and condominiums. People are returning to the downtown area to live.

Indianapolis prides itself as a home-and-family city, a place where the cost of living, the civic debt, and the crime rate are all below average. In fact, the National Municipal League has twice designated Indianapolis as an "All America City"—once in 1971 and again in 1982.

As Indianapolis accelerates into the future, there must be one more look at part of the city's past. It is preserved at the Indianapolis Motor Speedway and Hall of Fame Museum. The auto industry in the United States had an early start in central Indiana. In fact, the original purpose of the speedway was to serve as a test facility for the burgeoning auto industry. In 1898 the Haynes cars appeared in Kokomo, 50 miles to the north, as did the Apperson Jack Rabbit. The fever of building automobiles spread rapidly. The best-known Indianapolis products were the Cole (1909-25), the Marmon (1905-33), the Stutz (1912-36), the National (1903-24), the Pathfinder (1911-18), and the classic Duesenberg (1920-37).

Each of the museum's 500,000 annual visitors undoubtedly looks first for a Marmon driven by Ray Harroun, the 1911 winner of the "Indy 500." The collection includes 31 winning cars. Visitors see firsthand the advances made by the designers and mechanical wizards who created the open-cockpit, open-wheel marvels.

The most important development in speedway history is the emphasis on driver safety. Deaths were frequent when the solid-axle monsters, screaming at high speeds, hit concrete walls—the luckless driver absorbing 80 percent of the shock of impact. Twice in 1972, I gave the eulogy at funerals for my friends, drivers Art Pollard and Swede Savage. For me and thousands of race fans, these were tragic moments, which came all too frequently.

Since that year, however, dramatic improvements in car design and racing technology have reduced the risks, although the element of danger will always be present at high speeds. Only one fatality has occurred on the oval speedway in recent years—Gordon Smiley in 1982—even though qualifying speeds have increased by well over 25 miles per hour. Today's monocoque chassis absorbs 80 percent of the shock of a crash, just the opposite of the solid-axle creations of the Wilbur Shaw and Louis Meyer era. For the last few races, the thought of a fatality on the oval hasn't entered my mind. It's a healthy feeling. With qualifying speeds hovering around the

220-mile-per-hour mark, the race-car designers, engineers, and mechanics should draw cheers equal to those for the courageous drivers.

No matter how much we admire the machines, though, it is still the men who drive them that receive the most adulation—men like A.J. Foyt with four "500" wins; Bobby and Al Unser, Sr., with six wins between them; and Johnny Rutherford going for number four.

So it is with Indianapolis. Its new office buildings, hotels, museums, and sports arenas are awesome. However, the longest and loudest praise belongs to the men and women who years ago began to dream, who dared, who built, and who are still building an ideal community for families, businesses, culture,...and above all, for excitement.

Tom Carnegie

State Capitol Building (*above and facing*). Completed in 1888, the copper-domed capitol is one of the first large buildings ever constructed using Indiana limestone.

Courtrooms, State Capitol Building.

Soldiers and Sailors Monument (*above*). Completed in 1902, the 284-foot monument honors the Indiana citizens who died in the Civil War. Inside its cornerstone is a large copper box containing the names of the Indiana men who lost their lives in the conflict, a 38-star American flag, copies of daily and weekly newspapers from that era, and other related items. Extensive cleaning and restoration of the monument began in 1986. State Capitol Building (*facing*).

Hot-dog vendor (*facing*). Indiana National Bank Building and Christ Episcopal Church Cathedral (*above*). In 1838 the first church cornerstone in Indianapolis was laid when construction on the original Christ Church began. Two years later, Christ Church hosted the first church wedding in Indianapolis, the marriage of John Nowland and Amelia Smith. In 1857 work began on a new Christ Church building—a Gothic masterpiece built from Indiana limestone. The church was completed in 1860 and consecrated in 1862. Indianapolis skyline (*overleaf, pages 24-25*). In addition to the city's many cultural attractions and its designation as the "Amateur Sports Capital of the World," Indianapolis also places great emphasis on education. About a dozen institutions of higher learning are found in and near the city.

Police motorcycles with award plate (*above*). Building abstract in downtown (*facing*).

Union Station (*above and facing*). Carriage driver waits with "Bullet" for fares. When it opened in 1853, Union Station was the first union railway station in the country. In 1888 it was replaced by the present three-story, brick-and-granite, Romanesque Revival-style building.

Union Station (*above and facing*). After years of neglect, Union Station received a face-lift in a major restoration project. Reopened to the public with a flourish of 70,000 balloons in 1986 as a "festival marketplace," the station houses 107 retail shops, numerous restaurants and nightclubs, and a 276-room hotel. Thirteen hotel rooms are in 1920 Pullman cars located on the only remaining railroad track; each car contains two suites decorated with turn-of-the-century antiques. Seventy feet above the main floor of Union Station, five glass skylights illuminate the building's vaulted ceiling. Elegant arches and columns, terrazzo floors, and wrought-iron railings adorn the interior.

City Market Internationale (*above and facing*). Established in 1832 as a barter center for wood, hay, and farm goods, the original city market was replaced by a permanent structure in 1886. Today, the market is listed on the National Register of Historic Places and houses 56 tenants, serving an estimated 10,000 weekly visitors.

Conner Prairie (*below and facing*). A 55-acre museum complex owned and operated by Earlham College, the settlement contains 25 buildings, including pottery shops and working blacksmiths. Costumed interpreters depict life on the Indiana frontier during the 1830s.

Fruit and vegetable stand in Beanblossom (*below and facing*). Located about 40 miles south of Indianapolis, Beanblossom hosts an annual bluegrass music festival each summer. The town takes its name from a small creek that empties into the west fork of the White River.

Lockerbie Street (*above and facing*). Lockerbie Street bears the name of George Lockerbie, a well known citizen of Indianapolis in the early 1800s. The picturesque street was immortalized in verse by poet James Whitcomb Riley, who lived at 528 Lockerbie Street for 23 years until his death in 1916. Residential area northwest of downtown (*overleaf, pages 40-41*). When Indiana was admitted into the Union in 1816, its inhabitants included a large number of Scotch-Irish immigrants from Kentucky and Tennessee and two small pockets of French and Swiss settlers. After the Delaware and Miami Indians relinquished their rights to central and northern Indiana in 1818, more settlers arrived from Ohio, Virginia, and other southern states, including a large group of Quakers from North Carolina. By 1840 a German-Jewish community began to form in Indianapolis as a result of the large influx of German Jews to America in the mid-1800s.

Lockerbie Street (*above and facing*). James Whitcomb Riley Home (*overleaf, pages 46-47 and 48-49*). Known as the "Hoosier Poet," James Whitcomb Riley worked as a sign-painter before he began to write poetry for the Indianapolis *Journal* under the pseudonym "Benj. F. Johnson of Boone." He drew much of the material for his verses from rural and small-town life in Indiana. His Victorian home contains handcarved woodwork, ornate crystal chandeliers, turn-of-the-century antiques, unique baseboard drawers to hold shoes, and speaking tubes for communicating between the upstairs hallway and the kitchen.

President Benjamin Harrison Home (*above and facing*). A general during the Civil War and the nation's 23rd President, Benjamin Harrison made Indianapolis his home for most of his adult life. He is best known for having launched a modern U.S. Navy and for having started the American conservation movement during his term as President.

Crown Hill Cemetery (*above and facing*). Crown Hill Cemetery is one of America's largest cemeteries. President Benjamin Harrison, poet James Whitcomb Riley, and author Booth Tarkington, famous for his stories about middle-class American life set in Indiana, are buried here.

Indianapolis skyline from Crown Hill Cemetery (*above*). Electric streetcars connected Indianapolis to its suburbs as early as 1894. By 1900 they linked Indianapolis with other cities, such as Franklin, Muncie, and Lafayette. To capitalize on the new travel boom, streetcar companies opened up parks and amusement areas in places that could be reached by their cars. Monument Circle Building (*facing*). Through the years, Monument Circle has been the site of many festivities. One such occasion was a grand parade staged in 1927 to honor Charles Lindbergh, who was visiting Indianapolis after making his daring solo flight across the Atlantic Ocean. When the city decided to brick in Monument Circle in 1978, residents were given a chance to purchase bricks inscribed with their names for $25 each. Monument Circle Building was built on the site of the former J.C. Penney Building, which occupied the spot once held by English's Opera House.

Hoosier Dome (*above and facing*). The Indianapolis Colts are one of only six N.F.L. teams currently playing their home games in indoor stadiums. They signed a 20-year lease for use of the facility. Topping the $80 million, state-of-the-art structure is a 257-ton, air-supported, fiberglass roof rising 20 stories.

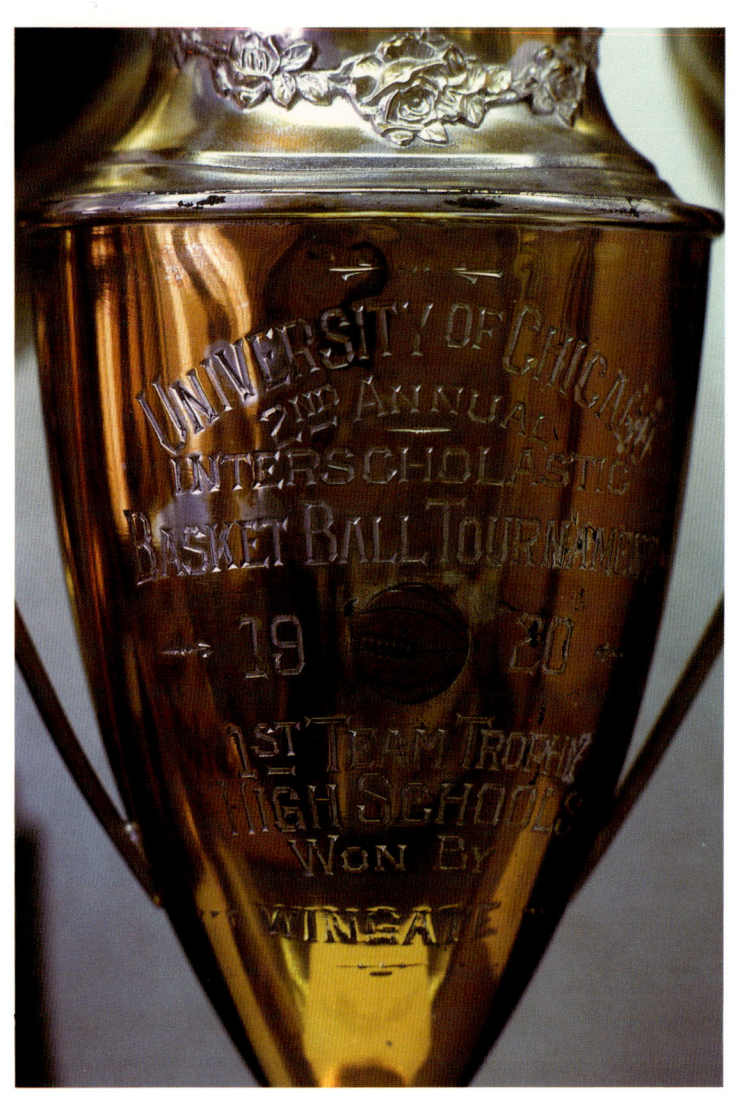

Indiana Basketball Hall of Fame (*above*). Boys' basketball game, Orchard School vs. Park Tudor School (*facing and overleaf, pages 60-61*). After World War II, Indianapolis basketball reached an all-time high, producing legendary teams and extraordinary coaches like Branch McCracken and John Wooden. Basketball remains a favorite with Indianapolis fans. When the N.B.A. staged its All-Star Game in the Hoosier Dome in 1985, it attracted 43,146 spectators — the largest crowd ever for such a game.

Indiana University Natatorium (*above and facing*). Called "the fastest pool in North America" by *Recreation, Sports & Leisure* magazine, the natatorium is the product of extensive research. Deep gutters along the edge collect waves generated by swimmers. Water is replenished up from the bottom rather than in from the sides. This design reduces turbulence and increases the speed of swimmers.

Major Taylor Velodrome (*above, facing, and overleaf, pages 64-65*). One of only 13 such facilities in the United States, the 333 1/3-meter velodrome hosts both national and international competitions. Racers on bikes with no brakes and only one gear can reach speeds of up to 55 miles per hour on the 28-degree banked, concrete surface. The track is named for Marshall "Major" Taylor, an Indianapolis native and champion cyclist in the early 1900s.

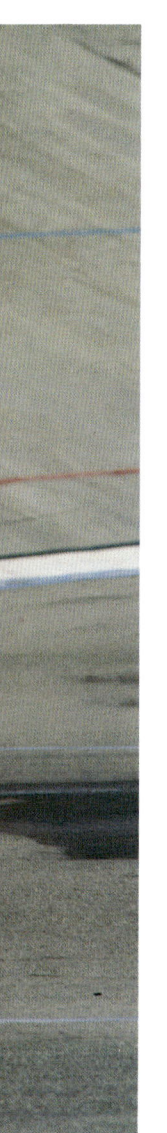

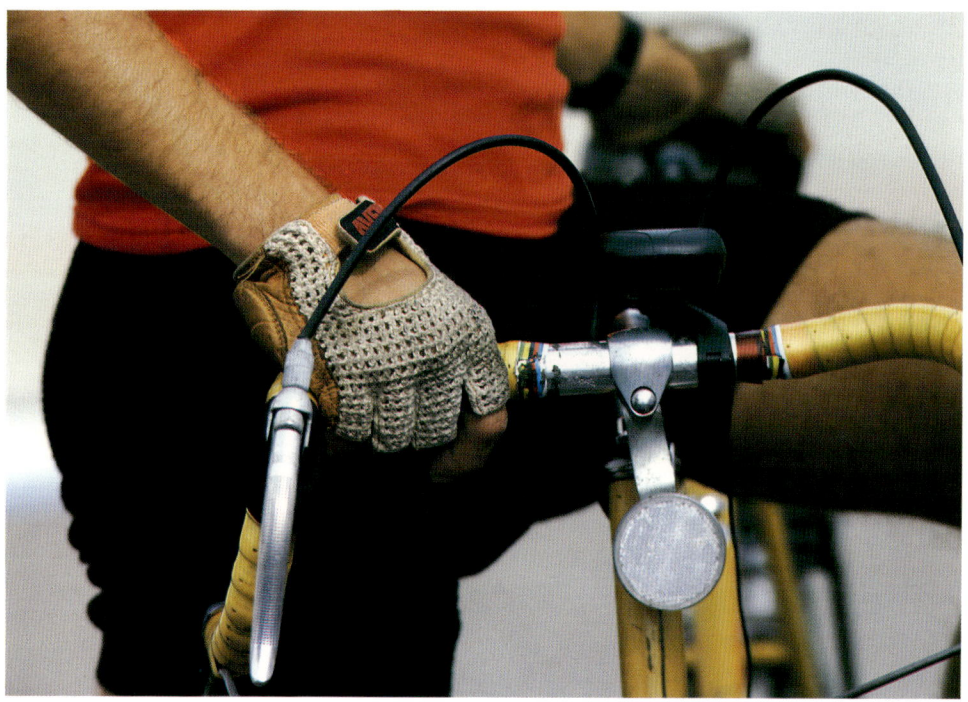

Park and canal, near Butler University (*above*). J.I. Holcomb Observatory at Butler University (*facing and overleaf, pages 70-71*). Called North Western Christian University until a name-change in 1877, Butler University has long had an international reputation in the performing arts, particularly in ballet. More than 4,000 students now attend the school, which bears the name of its benefactor, Ovid Butler.

William H. Block Company Building, corner of Illinois and Market Streets (*above*). Christmas tree-lighting ceremony, Circle Theatre (*facing*). The newly renovated, historic Circle Theatre on Monument Circle became the home of the Indianapolis Symphony Orchestra in 1984.

Indianapolis skyline (*above*). In 1822 residents of Indianapolis finally received regular U.S. mail service. Unless the waters of nearby rivers were swollen, the mail reached Indianapolis from the East every two weeks. Embassy Suites Hotel (*facing*).

State Capitol Building (*above*). Pro Patria Statue, World War Memorial Plaza (*facing*).

Indianapolis Ballet Theatre rehearsal at the Athenaeum, Michigan Avenue. When not on national tour, the Indianapolis Ballet performs for local residents at Clowes Memorial Hall, Butler University.

Indianapolis Museum of Art (*above and facing*). Located on the former estate of J.K. Lilly, the Museum of Art has the largest collection of J.M.W. Turner paintings outside the United Kingdom. It also houses the Eli Lilly collection of oriental art, one of the finest in the country.

Scottish Rite Cathedral (*above and facing*). Built in 1929, the ornate Tudor-Gothic cathedral has a 212-foot tower with a carillon of 54 bells. Inside the cathedral auditorium is a 5,000-pipe organ, supplemented by a 500-pipe echo organ. Indiana State Museum (*overleaf, pages 84-85*).

Hooks Historical Drugstore (*above, facing, and overleaf, pages 88-89*). Antique dental, medical, and pharmaceutical equipment are part of the exhibit at Hooks Historical Drugstore, along with a 19th-century soda fountain and candy counter.

The Children's Museum (*above and facing*). A merry-go-round is just one of the adventures awaiting visitors to The Children's Museum. Here children are encouraged to touch everything from animal skulls to bird feathers. They can ring bells, operate pulleys, or pretend they are sea captains with realistic props.

Racing-car tires (*facing*). After a car qualifies for the Indianapolis 500, its tires are impounded by officials until race day. Those same tires must then be put back on the car for the start of the race, because minute differences in tire diameter will affect the car's performance, especially at high speeds. Member of the Michael Andretti pit crew (*above*). Five mechanics work during each pit stop. Two of them fuel the car, while the others service the vehicle's tires. "Indy 500" race car (*overleaf, pages 94-95*). The fate of the "Indy 500" hung in the balance in 1945 when World War Ace and former driver Eddie Rickenbacker decided to sell the racing complex. The 570-acre facility was saved by the late Anton Hulman, Jr., a Terre Haute, Indiana, sportsman. Indianapolis Motor Speedway (*overleaf, pages 92-93*). More than 400,000 spectators fill the speedway on Memorial Day weekend, making the "Indy 500" race the most heavily attended single-day sporting event in the world.

Indianapolis Motor Speedway and Hall of Fame Museum (*below and facing*). The Speedway Museum's collection of classic, Indianapolis-manufactured cars includes the Cole (1909-25), the Marmon (1905-33), the Stutz (1912-36), the National (1903-24), the Pathfinder (1911-18), and the classic Duesenberg (1920-37). Union Station (*overleaf, pages 100-101*). Eagle Creek Reservoir (*overleaf, pages 102-103*). Located about ten miles from the center of town, Eagle Creek Reservoir is being developed into an internationally certified rowing course capable of accommodating world-championship rowing competition. Such a course needs to be straight and have no flow, two requirements the reservoir will meet.